# The Wild West in American History

# FRONTIERSMEN

**Written by Gail Stewart**
**Illustrated by Luciano Lazzarino**
**Edited by Mark E. Ahlstrom**

**LIBRARY OF CONGRESS**
**Library of Congress Cataloging-in-Publication Data**

Stewart, Gail, 1949-
    Frontiersmen  / by Gail B. Stewart.
      p.  cm. -- (The Wild West in American history)
    Summary: Discusses how the frontier in the United States moved west from
the thirteen original colonies after 1763 and what life was like for the courageous
people who chose to pursue the challenging existence of pioneers.
    ISBN 0-86625-406-4
    1. Frontier and pioneer life--United States--Juvenile literature.  2. Frontier and
pioneer life--West (U.S.)--Juvenile literature. 3. Pioneers--United States--History--
Juvenile literature. 4. Pioneers--West (U.S.)--History--Juvenile literature. 5. United
States--Territorial expansion--Juvenile literature.  6. West (U.S.)--History--Juvenile
literature. [1. Frontier and pioneer life.  2. United States--Territorial expansion.
3. West (U.S.)--History.] I. Title. II. Series.
E179.5.S83  1990
973--dc20                                                              89-37439
                                                                          CIP
                                                                          AC

**Rourke Publications, Inc.**
**Vero Beach, Florida, 32964**

# FRONTIERSMEN

# FRONTIERSMEN

Imagine what it might be like to live in a place far away from everything that is familiar to you. The nearest doctor would be hundreds of miles away. There would be no schools, and no stores. You would have to make your own clothes—even your own shoes. You would live in a small cabin, one that your family made by hand. Your meals would consist of the wild animals you could shoot or trap.

This new place would be filled with dangers. There would be ferocious grizzly bears and mountain lions on the prowl. There would be floods, blistering heat in the summer, and howling blizzards in the winter. Bands of hostile warriors would slip out of the shadows, attacking homes and murdering other settlers.

Life in this new place would never be easy. The weak or fearful would have difficulty surviving. Day-by-day living would require physical and mental toughness. Families and friends would need to stick together, to help one another out when there was trouble.

It's hard to imagine such a place, but it certainly existed. It's even more difficult to believe that thousands of people came to this place voluntarily. The life was hard, and there were many, many ways people could die in such a place. Yet this place was known by many who lived there as a "Paradise on Earth." It was the first American frontier—the "West." The people who risked their lives to live there were the first American pioneers, known as "frontiersmen."

# THE FIRST "WEST"

From the time of the first surge of Europeans to America, the country expanded in a westerly direction. The immigrants from England, Germany, Ireland, and France landed on the East Coast, and gradually pushed inland.

The original 13 American colonies along the Atlantic Coast were pretty much "settled" by the end of the 17th century. Towns and cities had been founded, and land for farms had been cleared. Most of the land had been "bought" (through some shady deals and agreements) from various tribes of Native Americans. For the most part, life in the 13 colonies ran smoothly.

No one had any idea how wide the country was. They knew that west of the colonies lay a vast range of mountains, called the Appalachians. Beyond the mountains, somewhere, lay the Pacific Ocean. The people living in the American colonies weren't sure how far away the ocean was—perhaps it was 200 miles, or 2,000 miles!

The frontier—the land that lay to the west of the settled territory of the colonies—was dense, dark forest. It was the first "West"—the territory that would later become the states of Kentucky, Ohio, Tennessee, and Indiana.

By its very nature, a frontier is unexplored land. It lies beyond the land that is already settled. For most of the colonists there was no reason at all to go into the unknown lands of the frontier. A few trappers and traders had ventured into the wilderness, but almost no one else. For the first 100 years of European settlement, therefore, the forests and mountains remained unsettled.

But for some people the very thought of a frontier was exciting. The tales and stories of hostile Indians and other dangers didn't seem to bother them. They wanted to set out at once. These were the frontiersmen.

**Only trappers and traders had ventured westward. (Art: Denver Public Library. Western History Dept.)**

# WHO WERE THEY?

**Boatloads of Europeans were arriving in Boston harbor. The immigrants were hoping for a better life.**

In the mid-1700's, many of the people who became frontiersmen were dissatisfied with life in the colonies. For them, the land was too settled, too tame. Many of these people talked about feeling hemmed in, for they felt that they were living too close to others. One frontiersman wrote in his journal that he figured when he could see smoke from another family's chimney, "people were just too crowded."

On the other hand, there were many frontiersmen who left civilization not to escape something bad, but to find something different or better. These were the people who yearned for the sight of new territory. They wanted to

find land where they could farm and hunt and raise their families.

Many of the frontiersmen had already been established on farms or in towns of the colonies. Historians tell us that in the mid-1700's there were more than one million Europeans living along the eastern coast of America. Some of these people were the first frontiersmen.

Yet there were others who came from Europe and set out directly for the frontier. They had heard of the rich soil and miles of woods. They were excited by a new land that no one had yet claimed. Nearly 500,000 more Europeans had arrived in America by 1770. They arrived in Boston harbor every week—boatloads of immigrants who could hardly wait to make a new life in America. Many of them set out for the American frontier.

By far, the greatest number of these immigrants had come from England, Scotland, and Ireland. They had endured discrimination because of their religion. Many had been farmers, trying desperately to scrape out a living on poor, rocky soil. To these people, the promise of acres and acres of rich soil, and forests thick with game, was a dream come true. In many ways, land was more of an incentive than money could ever have been. Land gave these people the dignity that they couldn't have in the farm country of England, Scotland, and Ireland.

# WHO OWNED THE FRONTIER?

When talking about these frontiersmen, it is easy to forget that they weren't Americans, at least not yet. All of the immigrants who settled in this country in the mid-1700's were colonists—they were living in a land owned by England. That made them British subjects.

There had been other nations besides England that had wanted a piece of this new land. France, for one, had tried to acquire large chunks of Canada and America. However, the French were forced to give up most of their holdings in 1763, after the British won the last of the French

and Indian Wars. The treaty signed between the two nations stated that all lands west of the settled colonies would be owned by England.

There were some people who were almost completely ignored when all this talk of land ownership was going on. The Native Americans, the various nations of Indians, had lived in the wilderness for thousands of years. Although they didn't "settle" the land in the way that white Europeans did, the Native Americans considered the land their own. They fished from its streams, they hunted game, and they planted corn. They took from the land only

**Native Americans had been living in North America for thousands of years.**

what they needed. Why, they thought, should they be forced from their own hunting grounds by armed bands of white European settlers?

The British knew that the Indians were capable of doing great harm to the colonists if they were angry. Having just won a series of long, bloody wars with the French, the British didn't want more violence. The French had been supported by the Native Americans—that's why the wars were called the French and Indian Wars.

# IGNORING ORDERS

# KING OF THE FRONTIERSMEN

*I*n 1763, King George III of England issued a proclamation called, appropriately, the Proclamation of 1763. His Highness made it strictly forbidden for settlers to go into the unsettled areas. That way there would be no frontiersmen who might stir up trouble with the Indians. Those settlers who had already claimed land, or who had bought land from Indians, had to give up the land and move back east, to "civilization."

The response from the settlers, however, wasn't what the king had in mind. Those who had ventured into the frontier, and who had found it every bit as wonderful as they had imagined, had no intention of going back east. They didn't feel any loyalty to England or the king. They felt no great loyalty to the colonies, either. They were stubborn and independent. Their loyalty was to their families and to their neighbors in the backwoods frontier.

Despite the king's order, a small trickle of new frontiersmen kept coming, too. They knew the British couldn't really enforce their rule—the king was, after all, thousands of miles across the ocean. Furthermore, no one really believed that British agents would want to tramp through the forests looking for frontiersmen.

As time went by, more and more settlers continued to move westward. Those who have studied the expansion of America say that in the 10 years that followed the Proclamation of 1763, the line of the frontier steadily moved westward—at the rate of 17 miles every year! Clearly, the urge to "go west" was far stronger in these people than the threat of punishment from the King of England.

One of the king's soldiers posts a copy of the Proclamation of 1763, forbidding settlement in new areas.

*O*ne of the most written-about figures of the 18th-century frontier was Daniel Boone. Boone had many different roles on the frontier. He was an explorer, a road builder, and a scout. He was a land dealer and a soldier, helping his fellow frontiersmen battle hostile Indian tribes. Most of all, Daniel Boone is famous for opening up the territory of Kentucky.

Boone was born in 1734 in Pennsylvania, but moved with his family to North Carolina when he was 15. He loved the wilderness, and often said he was never as happy as when he was on

**Daniel Boone**
**(Art: The Filson Club)**

an unfamiliar path in an unknown, unnamed territory. He was a skilled hunter and trapper. From his boyhood friendships with Indian children, he learned much about survival in the forest.

As a young man he heard stories about the land called Kentucky, or "Caintuck," as it was called by some early frontiersmen. There were forests so dense, according to the stories, that a man became invisible at a distance of 20 feet. It was said that horses would be stained with the red juice of wild strawberries—all the way up their legs—because the fruit grew so plentifully there. The game was supposed to be fat and slow and waiting to be hunted. Boone resolved that that was the place he wanted to be—even if the stories were only half true.

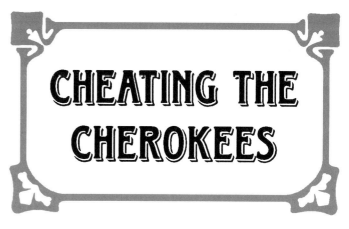

# CHEATING THE CHEROKEES

Over the next few years, Boone and a few of his friends made long trips into Caintuck. They were pleased with what they saw. Game was plentiful, and the soil looked like a

farmer's dream come true. Boone decided to move his family to the frontier. Together with six other families, the Boones moved in 1773. Along the way, Boone's young son James was tortured and killed by Indians. The tragedy frightened some of the travelers into going back to the settlements. The Boones, however, traveled on with some of the others and found a place to settle.

Two years later, Boone met a judge named Richard Henderson. Henderson was eager to purchase all of Kentucky from the Indians. His plan was to divide the land into parcels and sell them to people back east in the colonies. Henderson knew Daniel Boone was knowledgeable about the area, and he thought that Boone could help him with his land company, called Transylvania. (The name "Transylvania" means "across the woods.")

Although many different tribes lived in the vicinity of the Kentucky frontier, the Cherokees were the ones who finally sold the land to Henderson and his Transylvania Company. The history of American business dealings with the Native Americans had been one-sided, and Henderson's business was no different. For 10 wagonloads of tools, cloth, mirrors, beads, and whiskey, the Cherokees gave up all claims to the huge frontier of what is now all of Kentucky and part of Tennessee.

**Daniel Boone and his friends get the first view of "Caintuck."** *(Art: The Filson Club.)*

# BOONE'S TRACE

*D*aniel Boone's part in Henderson's scheme was to make it easy for new settlers to get to the frontier. The territory was rugged and extremely difficult to manage on foot, let alone with horses and wagons. How could families cross the mountains into Kentucky?

Those who had first made the hard journey through the mountains had used an ancient Indian path, called a "trace." (The word "trail" had not yet been used.) This trace had been explored in 1750 by a man from Virginia named Thomas Walker. Walker had named the trace, which led through a tiny gap in the mountains, the Cumberland Gap.

The trace through the Gap was no more than a few inches wide. The ground had been worn smooth by hundreds of moccasined feet over the centuries. The trace needed to be widened, though, so that more people could travel along it. That task fell to Daniel Boone.

With a crew of 28 men, Boone hacked a wide path from the settlements in Virginia all the way through the Cumberland Gap, right up to the shores of the Kentucky River. Armed with shining axes, the men cut down trees and cleared away underbrush. The finished road was called the Wilderness Road, or, simply, Boone's Trace. It provided an easier access to the new West—the frontier of Caintuck.

Besides the Wilderness Road, Boone and his crew built a fort in the frontier. Named Boonesboro, the fort provided some protection for the frontiersmen. For even though the Cherokees had "sold" Kentucky, tribes like the Shawnee and the Delaware hadn't agreed to the deal. As far as they were concerned, the Cherokees had no right to bargain with the white men. As far as they were concerned, the frontiersmen were an enemy to be driven away.

**Boone and his men carve a trail
through the Cumberland Gap.**

**An old drawing of Fort Boonesboro. *(Art: The Filson Club.)***

# FIGHTING TWO ENEMIES

It was not long afterward that the colonies went to war against England. This was the Revolutionary War, the one fought by the colonists to achieve their independence.

As we mentioned earlier, most of the people living on the backwoods frontier had no great loyalty to the colonies. In fact, the colonists hadn't been very cooperative about the needs of the frontiersmen. On more than one occasion, settlers had requested help in the form of supplies or arms, to help them fight off hostile Indians. No help was ever given, and the frontiersmen learned to fight however they could.

**George Rogers Clark made a special effort to get an emergency supply of gunpowder to the frontier.**

As it turned out, however, there were even fewer reasons to be loyal to the British. Most of the fighting was done throughout the settlements of the East, but the British weren't ignoring the frontiersmen. British officers were busily trying to get the Indians of the frontier to fight the new settlers. This plan seemed like a good one—the Americans would be fighting two enemies at the same time, the British and the Indians. Surely, they reasoned, the colonists could not win such a war.

George Rogers Clark, another famous frontiersman, came to the rescue. It was during the Revolution that he proved himself a real hero. A tall redhead from Virginia, Clark was keenly interested in the frontier. He knew the backwoodsmen were in need of help, and he intended to supply it.

On one occasion, he obtained 500 pounds of gunpowder and took it 400 miles to the Kentucky frontier. The gunpowder helped the settlers fight off the British troops and their Indian allies.

# THE HAIR BUYER

One of the most hated people in the Kentucky frontier was a British governor named Henry Harrison. Harrison presided over a British outpost in what is now the state of Indiana.

Harrison's key responsibility was to supply weapons to four of the largest tribes in the area. The Miamis, the Ottawas, the Shawnees, and the Delawares were all loyal to Harrison and the British. Those tribes, together with armed British troops, were making life almost unbearable for the settlers in Kentucky, Ohio, and Indiana.

Besides supplying the Indians with rifles and ammunition, Harrison offered them a special bonus. For every frontiersman's scalp the Indians could bring him, Harrison would pay a reward. The Indian could take as many goods and supplies from the outpost as he could hold in his two arms. This incentive led to a great many Indians scalping a great many frontiersmen. This also led to Harrison's gruesome nickname, "The Hair Buyer."

Harrison was captured, however, and locked in an American jail. His captor was George Rogers Clark, who sneaked up on the outpost with a handful of men. They used the secretive, quiet war strategy of the Indians, and beat them at their own game. Harrison's fort quickly surrendered. Clark's brave deeds were a big step toward ending the Indians' alliance with England.

**With only a handful of men, Clark was able to sneak up on the British outpost and capture "The Hair Buyer."**

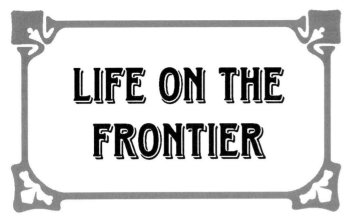

# LIFE ON THE FRONTIER

Most of the frontiersmen were not heroes like George Rogers Clark and Daniel Boone. Although they are not remembered by name, they were, nonetheless, important. They were the first to make a life in what was a dangerous, lonely place. What sort of lives did they lead?

We know from many journals and diaries kept by the frontiersmen that they left the settlements of the East with very little in the way of belongings. Many were very poor to start with, so they had few possessions. Others simply preferred not to carry heavy pieces of furniture and crates of bulky housewares over the Wilderness Road.

Many of the frontiersmen did bring livestock—usually a few pigs or sheep, and sometimes a cow. They also carried rifles and axes, two necessities in the frontier. The rifles would provide them with food and clothing—as well as offer protection from Indians and wild animals. The axes would clear land for farming.

It is important to understand one thing about the frontiersmen, and that is that they weren't all "men." In this book, we've decided to use the old term, rather than modify it to the more neutral-sounding "frontierspeople." The old term, however, refers to both men and women who lived and raised their families on the frontier. In most cases, the women had more jobs and responsibilities than their husbands had.

Women raised the children and helped their husbands with all of the farm chores. They prepared all the family's meals. They made all of the clothes the family wore, and they washed

and mended them. Women also knew how to handle a rifle, if need be.

The women of the frontier were hard-working and confident—they had to be. Many of the husbands were "long hunters," so named because they went off on long trips into the frontier searching for game. These hunting trips often lasted several months. During this time, the women had to hunt for the family's game, in addition to doing their other household chores.

When these frontier families left the settlements of the East, they knew they were leaving behind a way of life. On the frontier, their clothing, food, tools, homes—everything they needed—they would have to make themselves. There would be no going to a store for necessities or "extras." The frontiersmen—male and female—learned to rely on themselves. The frontier was a place where the strong had a chance of surviving. The weak had almost no chance at all. If they managed to stay alive, they usually turned around and headed back East!

**With few—if any—neighbors, life on the frontier could be very lonely. (Art: The Filson Club.)**

**In many ways, women were the real heroes of the frontier. They had to know how to do everything from cooking to hunting.**

# LINSEY-WOOLSEY AND BUCKSKIN

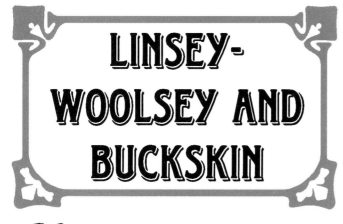

**C**lothing for the frontier family was usually made of deerskin or of fabric the women wove. The deerskin was, of course, provided by the abundant supply of deer in the forests. What wasn't used for clothing was often sold to traders from the East.

Selling deerskin was one of the few ways the frontiersmen could earn money. Money was certainly in short supply in the backwoods, and there weren't many ways to spend it. There were a few items, however, that simply couldn't be made or grown by the frontiersmen. Gunpowder, lead for bullets, and other pieces of metal for tools had to be purchased from traders. Deerskin from a doe was worth about 50 cents in the late 18th century. The skin of a buck, which was larger, was worth a dollar. (This, by the way, is where we get the slang term "buck," meaning one dollar.)

A man living on the frontier might wear pants and a shirt made of deerskin for hunting or trapping. Deerskin, however, wasn't very comfortable. It tended to get clammy when it got wet, and it was stiff when it dried. Clothes made of a combination of linen and wool were far more comfortable.

The linen came from a plant called flax, which was grown by almost all the frontiersmen. The flax was harvested, and the stiff reeds were left in wet piles to rot. After they rotted, the strong fibers inside the reeds were exposed.

The process of making flax fibers into linen thread, and finally weaving the thread into fabric, was a long one. The end result—smooth, creamy linen—was usually combined with wool

**Making linsey-woolsey was very time consuming. The yarn was made on a spinning wheel.**

yarn, made from the family's sheep. This material was called linsey-woolsey, and was stronger and more durable than pure wool. Underwear, shirts, and petticoats were all made of linsey-woolsey.

Sometimes the material was dyed by using natural colorings. Oak bark, for example, produced a strong black color, and walnut bark made a deep brown. Certain types of ash trees produced a blue dye. Linsey-woolsey that wasn't dyed was a yellowish-white in color.

# SHOES FULL OF LEAVES

The moccasins, made of deerskin, came up about 10 inches on the leg. Like any deerskin apparel, they were uncomfortable when wet, but they at least offered some protection from stones and sharp roots on the ground. In the winter, the moccasins were stuffed with dried leaves or deer hair, as a way of insulating them.

*M*ost frontiersmen went barefoot whenever possible. Boots and shoes were almost nonexistent. Historians tell us that the frontiersmen could always tell newcomers from the East because they wore boots! Footwear wore out quickly in the rugged terrain of the frontier, and when it did, it had to be replaced. When footwear was needed, the frontiersmen usually wore moccasins.

**After putting up a temporary "half-camp," the first order of business on the frontier was to clear land for crops.**

# GETTING SETTLED

Some of those who came to the frontier did so because they had already bought land from a dealer. However, there were many frontiersmen who just "showed up" in the backwoods of Kentucky or Tennessee. When they found land that was unsettled, they stopped their journey. These frontiersmen simply "staked their claim" by building a home and clearing some land for farming.

In the days of the early frontier, living on the land was almost as good as having a deed or title. This kind of frontiersman was called a "squatter." Many of the squatters went on to register their land later, after the government had measured, or "surveyed," the land.

Frontiersmen tried to time their journey so that they would reach their land in the late spring. That way, there would be time to get in crops of corn and flax that could be harvested in the late summer. The planting couldn't wait, so they didn't want to waste any time by building a cabin.

What they did was to put up a temporary "half-camp." The half-camp was a rectangular structure, which was open on one side. It was built of slender branches and logs. The open side faced a fire that burned all the time, day and night. The family could live in it until the weather turned cold, or until there was enough time to build a good, strong cabin.

# THE FRONTIER CABIN

*W*hile the half-camp took only several hours to build, the family log cabin was a much harder job. It was often built by a group of neighbors, working together. Such an event was called a "houseraising." Large jobs, such as building a house, were far easier when several people worked together. It was also a chance for friends and relatives to get together and have some fun, as well as to work.

In the case of a houseraising, the neighbors would gather when the frontiersman and his family had a site prepared, and logs already cut. Then the houseraising would begin. When work was over for the day, there would be drinking, eating, and having fun. In the end, the houseraising resulted in a strong log home.

The cabin was built out of carefully selected trees. Trees of less than 10 inches around were considered too small. The trees were all cut and

A "houseraising" on the frontier was an occasion for neighbors to get together and help one another. When the work was done, they could relax.

shaped with only an ax. No other tools for housebuilding really existed on the frontier. Cabins built in the early frontier days were built without nails. Everything was notched or fastened with wood pegs.

The logs were notched, or tapered, at the ends, so that they fit snugly at the corners. Stacking and fitting the logs for the walls was heavy work, and it's hard to imagine anyone doing the job without the help of neighbors. The women and children did the job called "chinking"—filling in the spaces between the logs. By packing peat, mud, or moss between the logs, the frontiersmen would have a cabin that would be more airtight. There would be less chance of cold, drafty winds, snow, and rain blowing through the walls.

The finished cabin was usually about 20 feet long and 16 feet wide. There was a stone fireplace and hearth at one end. The furnishings were pretty meager—a homemade table and some stools, a bed made of wood planks, a loft where the children slept, and maybe a cradle made out of a log. A pair of deer antlers fastened to the wall made a good gun rack or set of hooks.

Log cabins on the frontier were quite dark—especially during the day, when there was no fire on the hearth. There were no real windows in the cabin, for glass was only found in cities and towns. Some cabins had shutters that could be opened to let in a little light and breeze. These were shut and bolted tight at night, to keep out any unfriendly Indians who might be lurking nearby.

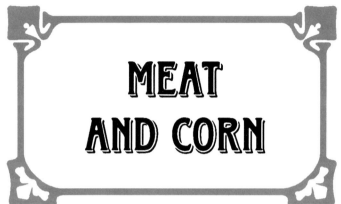

# MEAT AND CORN

The frontiersmen usually had plenty to eat, but there wasn't a great deal of variety. The basis of their diet was meat and corn. The meat came from the forests filled with game—buffalo, rabbit, deer, bear, panther, and so on. The corn was grown in the rich soil near the cabin. Corn, or "maize," had been grown for hundreds of years by Native Americans. It was they who showed the first Europeans in America how to grow it.

The corn was eaten in many different ways. Ears were roasted; dried corn was ground into meal. Everyone ate corn soup, corn pone, and corn bread. Corn mush was eaten at breakfast, topped with milk or bear grease.

The settlers had no way of refrigerating their food, so they had to preserve it in other ways. Milk from the family cow was often drunk sour—the fronstiersmen liked sour milk, luckily. It was never cold. Meat was usually dried in long strips and smoked over a fire. The dried meat, called "jerky," would keep for a long time.

Another important way of preserving meat was by salting it. The frontiersman used a great

deal of salt—not as a seasoning as we do today, but as a means of keeping meat from spoiling. A frontier family would soak the meat in brine water, which is water heavily doused with salt. Then the meat would be hung up to dry. The meat looked and tasted much like the dried beef we have today.

Frontier salt came from certain natural mineral springs. These springs were favorite gathering places for wild animals. They liked to come and lick the salt that formed around the spring. For that reason, such natural salt springs were called "salt licks." The first frontier towns were usually built near one of these salt licks. They were as important as a good water supply. The settlers sometimes named their town after the person who discovered that particular lick, such as Miller's Lick or Carson's Lick. Even today, there are many little towns in Kentucky, Tennessee, and Indiana that still have the work "Lick" in their names!

# ONLY THE BEGINNING

This first frontier was the initial push by settlers into the American continent. As more and more people ventured into the wilderness, the traces became worn, and widened into roads.

Pretty soon, it wasn't a frontier anymore. The backwoods of Indiana, Kentucky, Tennessee, and Ohio became more and more settled. This made many frontiersmen head west again—to the Mississippi. As that territory became more populated, the frontier was pushed to the Rocky Mountains, and then the California coast.

The pioneers who made each new push had learned from the frontiersmen before—ways of building homes, making clothes, and dealing with the dangers of the frontier. Those who tackled this "first West," the frontier on the other side of the Appalachians, probably had no idea what they were starting!

**On the frontier, meat had to be preserved either by smoking it over a fire or by soaking it in brine.**

# ADELIA AND OLD TICK-LICKER

*N*o book about the American frontier would be complete without mentioning the Kentucky rifle. A rifle was considered basic equipment on the frontier. With it, a frontiersman obtained food and clothing. It was with his rifle that a frontiersman could earn a little money shooting deer and selling deerskins. In addition, the rifle gave the frontiersman protection against Indians.

Frontiersmen depended so much on their rifles that they almost always gave them pet names. They'd carve the name into the wooden part of the rifle, or on the brass plate on the stock. The names were usually elaborate feminine names, common in that day. Modern gun collectors have found rifles from the 1700's with such names as "Eulalia" and "Adelia."

Daniel Boone, for reasons unknown, called his trusty rifle "Old Tick-Licker"!

There was a particular type of rifle that almost all frontiersmen used. The settlers of the early frontier needed a gun different from the ones available to them. Muskets, used by soldiers and a few hunters in the East, weren't accurate except at close range. Other rifles of that time were very difficult to load. One rifle, the Jaeger, was especially hard to load—the only way the bullets could be loaded was by hammering on the ramrod with a mallet!

Needless to say, the American frontiersman needed a gun that would be reliable and accurate. And because of the many dangers he faced, he needed a rifle that could be loaded quickly and easily.

Gunsmiths in Lancaster, Pennsylvania, developed such a rifle. It was almost five feet long, but fairly light. It was amazingly accurate at almost unheard-of distances. A frontiersman would have little trouble bringing down a deer at 300 yards. A musket of those days, on the other hand, could shoot only 150 yards— and very inaccurately, at that.

The "secret" of this new rifle, besides its extra-long barrel, was that it had tiny grooves inside the barrel. Other guns were smooth on the inside. The grooves of the Kentucky rifle controlled the "ball," or bullet. The grooves made the ball spin when it was fired, and that made the rifle shoot true. The frontiersmen liked this rifle from Pennsylvania, and almost every man setting out for the Kentucky frontier owned one. For that reason, the gun has been known as the "Kentucky rifle" for many years.

The wooden outside of the gun, called the stock, was usually made of maple or walnut. The stock was polished over and over until it was as smooth as tortoise shell. In the underside of the barrel was an indentation. This was where the frontiersman stored the ramrod, an important part of the rifle. The ramrod was made of hickory wood, and was used to force the lead balls deep into the barrel.

The lead balls fired by the Kentucky rifle were quite small. This meant that they could be made more cheaply, and that the frontiersman would need less gunpowder to shoot them. Many of the early frontiersmen made their own balls in a metal mold. Hot lead was poured into the mold, and when it cooled, the balls were removed from the mold. Some molds made 10 or 12 balls at a time.

Loading the Kentucky rifle took about a minute for an experienced shooter. First, he had to measure out a certain amount of gunpowder from the cow's horn he wore around his neck. He poured the powder into the opening of the bore, called the muzzle. The next step was to take out a lead ball and, with the ramrod, insert it into the muzzle. Because these bullets were so small, frontiersmen wrapped each one in a greased patch made of cloth or leather before stuffing it into the muzzle of the rifle. The snug fit made the bullet fire more accurately. Finally, the frontiersman primed the firing mechanism with a little more gunpowder, and cocked the rifle. As soon as it was cocked, the Kentucky rifle was ready to fire.

**The Kentucky rifle—along with balls, powder, and patches—was basic equipment for the frontiersman.**

# IN THE DAYS OF THE FRONTIERSMEN

| | |
|---|---|
| 1620 | The English ship *Mayflower* lands in Massachusetts. |
| 1732 | George Washington is born in the Virginia territory. |
| 1733 | A huge epidemic of influenza rages through New York City and Philadelphia. |
| 1734 | Daniel Boone is born in Pennsylvania. |
| 1745 | French troops and their Indian allies attack British settlements in Maine. |
| 1768 | The Indiana Company buys almost two million acres of land from the Iroquois Indians. The land lies southwest of the Ohio River. |
| 1770 | The first rhubarb is shipped from London to the United States by Benjamin Franklin. |
| 1773 | The Boston Tea Party occurs. |
| 1775 | Thomas Paine publishes an article supporting the rights of women. |
| 1776 | The Declaration of Independence is signed in Philadelphia. |
| 1778 | The first peace treaty between Americans and Native Americans is signed. |
| 1783 | The *Pennsylvania Evening News* becomes America's first daily newspaper. |
| 1788 | A huge fire in New Orleans wipes out 19 city blocks and more than 850 homes. |
| 1790 | The U.S. population is 3,929,214. |
| 1794 | The first U.S. silver dollar is minted. |
| 1796 | Tennessee becomes the 16th state. |
| 1797 | John Adams is inaugurated as the second U.S. president. |
| 1801 | Thomas Jefferson becomes the third U.S. president. |
| 1803 | Explorers Lewis and Clark set off on their expedition to see the lands recently purchased from France. |
| 1804 | The first shipment of bananas comes to the United States from Latin America. |
| 1806 | Shoemakers in Philadelphia organize a huge strike. |
| 1808 | Congress prohibits the African slave trade. |
| 1809 | James Madison becomes the nation's fourth president. |
| 1810 | There are 366 newspapers in the United States. |
| 1812 | Louisiana becomes the 18th state. |